2-04

BK

W9-BKC-912

Predators in the Wild

Grizzly Bears

by Kathleen W. Deady

Consultant:

Kimberly S. McGrath

Executive Director

The American Bear Association

CAPSTONE
HIGH-INTEREST
BOOKS

an imprint of Capstone Press
Mankato, Minnesota

Capstone High-Interest Books are published by Capstone Press
151 Good Counsel Drive, P.O. Box 669, Mankato, Minnesota 56002
http://www.capstone-press.com

Library of Congress Cataloging-in-Publication Data
Deady, Kathleen W.
    Grizzly bears/by Kathleen W. Deady.
    p. cm.—(Predators in the wild)
    Includes bibliographical references and index (p. 32).
    Summary: Describes grizzly bears, their habits, where they live, their
hunting methods, and how they exist in the world of people.
    ISBN 0-7368-1063-3
    1. Grizzly bear—Juvenile literature. [1. Grizzly bear. 2. Bears.] I.Title.
II. Series.
QL737.C27 D42 2002
599.784—dc21   2001002925

Editorial Credits
Blake Hoena, editor; Karen Risch, product planning editor; Timothy Halldin,
    cover designer and illustrator; Katy Kudela, photo researcher

Photo Credits
Erwin and Peggy Bauer, 11, 15, 22
Erwin and Peggy Bauer/TOM STACK & ASSOCIATES, 6
Joe McDonald, 8, 12, 20
John Gerlach/Visuals Unlimited, 17 (upper left)
Kent and Donna Dannen, 27
Mark Newman/TOM STACK & ASSOCIATES, cover
Robert McCaw, 29
Robin Brandt, 10, 14, 17 (lower left)
Steve Callahan/Visuals Unlimited, 17 (lower right)
Tom Edwards/Visuals Unlimited, 24
Unicorn Stock Photos/Mark and Sue Werner, 9, 18, 21
Victoria Hearst/TOM STACK & ASSOCIATES, 16
Will Troyer/Visuals Unlimited, 17 (upper right)

1 2 3 4 5 6 07 06 05 04 03 02

Table of Contents

Common names:	Grizzly bear, grizzly, brown bear, white bear, silvertip
Scientific name:	*Ursus arctos horribilis*
Length:	Grizzlies usually are 6 to 8 feet (1.8 to 2.4 meters) long.
Height:	Grizzlies are 3 to 5 feet (.9 to 1.5 meters) high at the shoulders. They may be 6 to 10 feet (1.8 to 3 meters) tall when standing upright.
Weight:	Male grizzlies usually weigh between 350 and 700 pounds (159 and 318 kilograms). Females usually weigh between 250 and 350 pounds (113 to 159 kilograms).
Life span:	Grizzlies live an average of 25 years.

Appearance: Grizzlies can be brown, black, or blond. They have silver-tipped hairs on the back and shoulders.

Habitat: Most grizzlies live in Alaska and Canada. They live in mountainous areas with forests, river valleys, and meadows.

Prey: Grizzlies are omnivores. They eat both plants and animals. They eat grasses, roots, nuts, berries, flowers, and honey. They also eat insects and small animals such as lizards and fish.

Eating habits: Grizzlies eat large amounts of food. They may eat as much as 100 pounds (45 kilograms) each day during the fall.

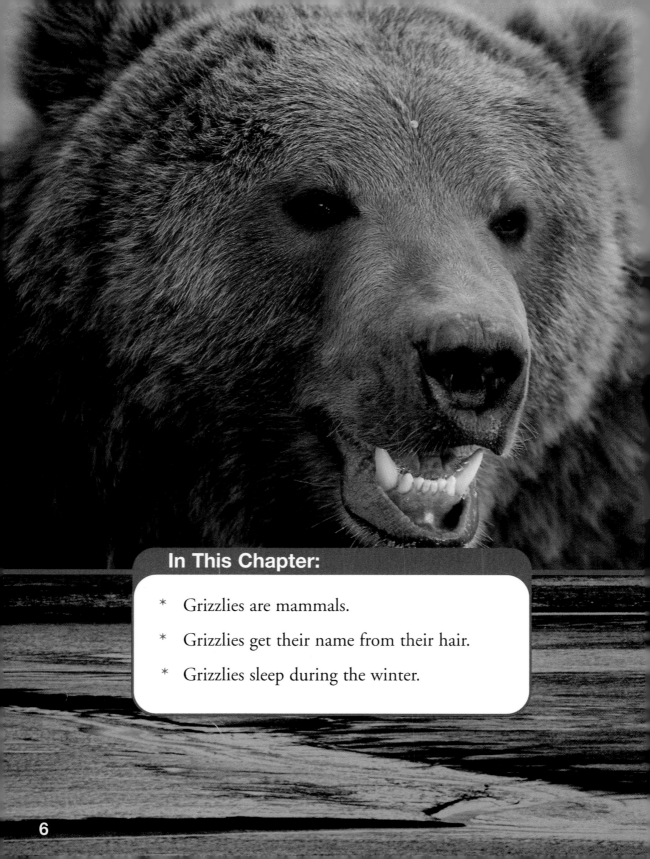

In This Chapter:

* Grizzlies are mammals.

* Grizzlies get their name from their hair.

* Grizzlies sleep during the winter.

Chapter 1

Grizzly Bears

Grizzly bears are one of the largest land animals. They can weigh more than 1,000 pounds (450 kilograms). They can be 10 feet (3 meters) tall when standing upright.

Some people think grizzlies are slow and clumsy because of their large size. But grizzlies can run up to 35 miles (56 kilometers) per hour over short distances. They also can change directions quickly when running.

Grizzlies are very strong. They are one of the most powerful predators on land. They can kill even large prey with one blow from their paws.

Mammals

Grizzlies are mammals. Mammals are warm-blooded. They maintain a steady body temperature. Mammals also have hair and give live birth to their young.

Scientists divide mammals into groups called orders. Bears belong to the order Carnivora. Animals in this group eat other animals. This group also includes lions, tigers, and wolves.

Bear Species

Bears belong to the family Ursidae. This scientific group includes eight bear species. A species is a specific type of animal or plant.

Brown bears are one bear species. Several brown bear subspecies also exist. Subspecies are closely related animals. But they often live in different geographical areas. Two brown bear subspecies live in North America. These bears are grizzly bears and Kodiak bears.

Appearance

Grizzly bears have thick fur. Their fur can be brown, black, or blond. They have silver-tipped hair on the back and shoulders. People gave grizzlies their name because of these hairs. The hairs give them a "grizzled" appearance.

Grizzlies have silver-tipped hair on the back and shoulders.

People also gave grizzlies the nickname "silvertip" because of these hairs.

Grizzlies have a large, bulky body. They have a hump of muscle and fat on their shoulders. They have a large head, rounded ears, and a short tail. Grizzlies have short, strong legs and flat feet. These features allow them to stand upright.

Female grizzlies protect their cubs.

Size

Grizzly bears can vary greatly in size. Male grizzlies are larger than females. They usually weigh between 350 and 700 pounds (159 and 318 kilograms). Females weigh between 250 and 350 pounds (113 and 159 kilograms).

Most grizzlies are 6 to 8 feet (1.8 to 2.4 meters) long. They are 3 to 5 feet (.9 to 1.5 meters) tall when standing on all four feet. They may be 6 to 10 feet (1.8 to 3.0 meters) tall when standing upright.

Cubs

Grizzlies are solitary animals. They usually hunt and live alone. But grizzlies gather together in June and July to find a mate.

Between January and March, a female gives birth to as many as four cubs. The cubs stay with the mother for two or three years. She teaches them hunting skills. She also protects them from predators such as mountain lions and wolves.

Cubs

Grizzly bears usually sleep in a den during the winter. Sleeping helps them survive the lack of food during the cold months. Cubs are born while the female sleeps. The cubs weigh less than 1 pound (.5 kilograms) at birth.

In spring, the female and the cubs leave the den. By then, the cubs weigh about 20 pounds (9 kilograms).

In This Chapter:

* Grizzlies are omnivores.

* Grizzlies eat more during the summer and fall.

* Grizzlies have an excellent sense of smell.

The Hunt

Grizzly bears are omnivores. They eat both plants and animals. They eat grasses, roots, nuts, berries, and flowers. They eat insects. Grizzlies also eat lizards, fish, and other small animals.

Diet

Grizzly bears' diets depend on the food available. They may graze on grasses, fruits, berries, and nuts. They also dig up plant roots. They find bees and honey in beehives.

Grizzlies that live near water often eat fish.

Grizzlies are excellent hunters. They turn over rocks and logs in search of insects and lizards. They hunt for mice, squirrels, and many other small animals. Grizzlies that live near water eat many kinds of fish.

Grizzlies also prey on the young of larger animals. These animals include deer, elk, moose, and bison.

Grizzlies eat almost anything. Grizzlies even eat the decaying flesh of dead animals. This flesh is called carrion.

Claws and Teeth

Grizzly bears have five curved claws on each paw. The front paws' claws may be as long as 4 inches (10 centimeters). Grizzlies use their claws to dig and to catch prey.

Grizzlies have very powerful jaws. They have 42 teeth. Sharp, pointed canine teeth in the front help them hold and kill prey. Flat molars in the back help them grind and chew food.

Eating Habits

A grizzly's diet varies with the seasons. In spring, a grizzly may eat 25 to 35 pounds (11 to 16 kilograms) of food each day. In the summer and fall, it eats more to prepare for winter. A grizzly may eat nearly 100 pounds (45 kilograms) of food each day. It may gain as much as 400 pounds (181 kilograms).

Standing

Grizzlies may stand upright. They do this to get a better look at their surroundings.

Senses

Scientists believe that grizzlies see as well as people can. They believe grizzlies can see forms, movements, and colors. Grizzlies also can see well at night.

Grizzlies have an excellent sense of smell. They can smell carrion that is 1 mile (1.6 kilometers) away. Female grizzlies use their sense of smell to find their cubs if the cubs get lost. Grizzlies also use their sense of smell to find a mate.

Grizzlies hear well. They can hear soft sounds such as a twig snapping 200 yards (183 meters) away. This ability helps them know if prey is nearby. Scientists think grizzlies may be able to hear high-pitched sounds that people cannot hear.

What Grizzly Bears Eat

Small mammals

Fish

Young moose

Berries

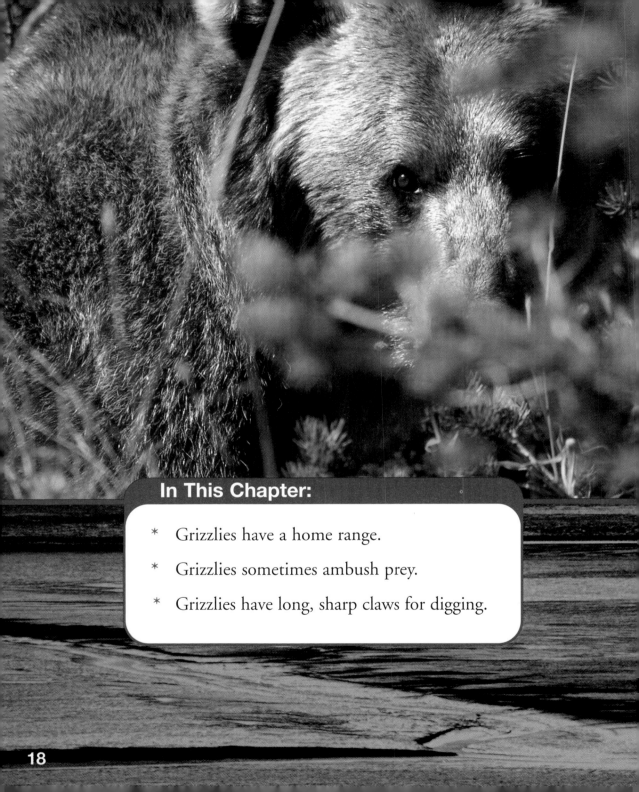

In This Chapter:

*   Grizzlies have a home range.

*   Grizzlies sometimes ambush prey.

*   Grizzlies have long, sharp claws for digging.

The Kill

Grizzlies defend a home range. They move around this area to find food, a mate, and raise their young.

The size of the range varies greatly with the amount of food available. Ranges are smaller where food is plentiful. Along the coast, a bear can find plenty of fish. A grizzly then may only need a range that is 10 to 12 square miles (26 to 31 square kilometers). In the mountains, a grizzly may need a larger area. Prey is harder to find there. A grizzly that lives in the mountains may have a home range that is 500 square miles (1,295 square kilometers).

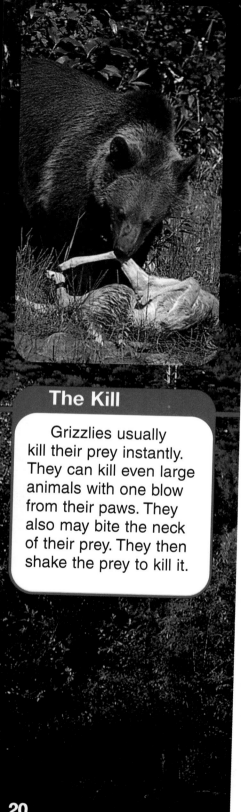

The Kill

Grizzlies usually kill their prey instantly. They can kill even large animals with one blow from their paws. They also may bite the neck of their prey. They then shake the prey to kill it.

Larger Prey

Grizzly bears seldom hunt large prey such as moose, elk, or bison. But when they do, they usually hunt young, old, and sick animals. These animals are easier to catch and kill than healthy adult animals.

Grizzlies sometimes ambush large prey. They hide along a trail and wait for prey to pass by. They then attack the prey from behind and drag it to the ground. Grizzlies also may attack prey crossing a stream or running through snow. It is more difficult for the prey to escape during these times.

Smaller Prey

Grizzly bears eat many small animals such as squirrels, mice, and gophers. These animals sometimes try to

Grizzlies turn over rocks to look for prey.

escape into an underground burrow. Grizzlies then use their claws to dig into the ground and reach the animals.

Grizzlies also forage for insects and lizards. They use their long claws to tear apart rotten logs to find insects. They turn over rocks to look for insects and lizards.

Camping

Campers should be careful when camping in bear habitats. Campers should hang their food in trees out of reach of bears. They also can store food in bear-proof containers. Campers should not eat near their sleeping area. Bears may smell the food remains and wander near the sleeping area.

Fishing

Grizzly bears use several methods to catch fish. Grizzlies sometimes stand in the shallow water below waterfalls. Fish may gather in these areas. Grizzlies grab the fish with their claws when they come close.

Grizzlies may even pounce on fish. They push the fish against the bottom of the riverbed when they do this. They then stick their head underwater and grab the fish.

Grizzlies also wade into shallow water at the top of a waterfall. Some fish travel up stream to spawn. They may have to jump over waterfalls to reach a place to lay their eggs. Grizzlies wait for the fish to jump up the waterfalls. They catch the fish in midair with their teeth.

Myth: Grizzlies cannot run downhill.

Fact: Grizzlies can run uphill or downhill quickly and easily.

Myth: Grizzlies have very poor eyesight.

Fact: Grizzlies can see as well as people can. They also can see well at night.

Myth: Grizzlies are fierce hunters and attack people.

Fact: Grizzlies often avoid people. But, a grizzly may attack if surprised or to protect its cubs.

In This Chapter:

* Most grizzly attacks can be prevented.

* Fewer grizzlies exist today than in the past.

* Predators kill close to half of grizzly cubs.

Chapter 4

In the World of People

Many people fear grizzly bears. Early settlers believed that grizzlies were bloodthirsty killers. Even today, many people think grizzlies will attack for no reason.

Grizzlies rarely are a threat to people. They seem to avoid people whenever possible. But grizzlies can be dangerous. Attacks do happen.

Range

Today, grizzly bears live mainly in Alaska and western Canada. But they once lived in most of western North America.

In the early 1800s, about 100,000 grizzlies lived in North America. Half of these bears lived south of Canada. Today, less than 50,000 grizzlies are left. Fewer than 1,000 grizzlies live south of Canada. These bears live in Wyoming, Montana, Idaho, and Washington.

In 1975, scientists listed grizzlies as a threatened species south of Canada. Grizzlies are in danger of dying out there.

Preventing Grizzly Bear Attacks

Grizzly bears seldom attack people. But they may attack if surprised or threatened. A female grizzly may attack a person who gets between her and her cubs.

People should warn grizzlies of their presence. They may talk and make loud noises as they hike through bear habitats. Some hikers wear bells or shake stones in cans. Grizzlies usually avoid people. They move away when they hear human noises.

Grizzlies may approach campers for food. Many people store their food in bear-proof containers. Others hang their food out of the reach of bears.

People should never feed bears. Grizzlies then may become used to human food and lose their fear of people. They may wander into towns looking for food. The grizzlies may attack people in the towns. These grizzlies often are killed to keep people safe.

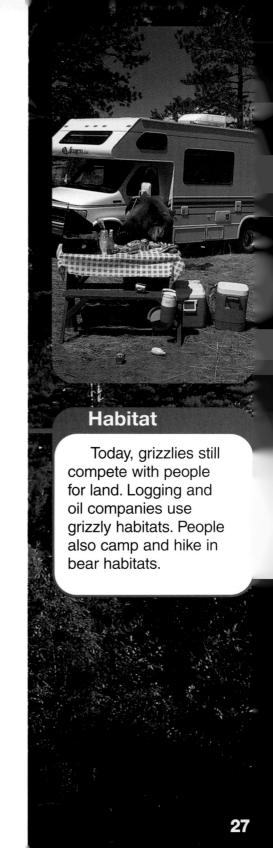

Habitat

Today, grizzlies still compete with people for land. Logging and oil companies use grizzly habitats. People also camp and hike in bear habitats.

Threats to Grizzlies

Grizzly bears are large, powerful animals. No other predator hunts adult grizzlies as prey. But predators such as wolves may attack and kill grizzly cubs.

The largest threat to grizzlies is the loss of habitat. In the 1800s, settlers moved west in large numbers. They built towns and began farming land where grizzlies lived. Grizzlies began to lose their habitat and food sources.

Many people killed grizzlies. Farmers killed grizzlies to protect their farm animals. Some people killed grizzlies out of fear. Others hunted grizzlies for sport.

Protecting Grizzlies

Today, it is illegal to hunt grizzly bears. But hunters sometimes kill grizzlies by accident. They may mistake them for black bears. People are allowed to hunt black bears.

Scientists are concerned about the number of grizzlies in the wild. Grizzlies breed slowly. A female may have young only every three or four years. Predators kill about 40 percent of grizzly cubs. Grizzlies are dying faster than they can replace themselves.

Loss of habitat is the biggest threat to grizzlies' survival.

Many people are working to protect grizzlies. Several national organizations teach people about grizzlies. They tell people about the dangers to grizzlies. They also tell people how to avoid bear attacks. With these efforts, grizzlies should continue to survive in the wild.

ambush (AM-bush)—to hide and then attack prey

carrion (KARE-ee-uhn)—dead animal flesh

forage (FOR-ij)—to search for food

habitat (HAB-uh-tat)—the place and natural conditions in which plants and animals live

mammal (MAM-muhl)—a warm-blooded animal with a backbone; mammals also have hair and give live birth.

omnivore (OM-nuh-vor)—an animal that eats both plants and other animals

predator (PRED-uh-tur)—an animal that hunts other animals for food

range (RAYNJ)—the area where an animal lives and hunts

solitary (SOL-uh-ter-ee)—living and hunting alone; bears are solitary animals.

species (SPEE-sheez)—a specific type of animal or plant

To Learn More

Bair, Diana, and Pamela Wright. *Bear Watching.* Wildlife Watching. Mankato, Minn.: Capstone High-Interest Books, 2000.

Kallen, Stuart A. *Grizzly Bears.* Checkerboard Animal Library. Edina, Minn.: Abdo & Daughters, 1998.

Leach, Michael. *Grizzly Bear: Habitats, Life Cycles, Food Chains, Threats.* Natural World. Austin, Texas: Raintree Steck-Vaughn, 2001.

Stone, Jason, and Jody Stone. *Grizzly Bear.* Wild Bears. Woodbridge, Conn.: Blackbirch Press, 2000.

Useful Addresses

Canadian Wildlife Service
Environment Canada
Ottawa, ON K1A 0H3
Canada

National Wildlife Federation
11100 Wildlife Center Drive
Reston, VA 20190

Grizzly Discovery Center
P.O. Box 996
West Yellowstone, MT 59758

North Cascades National Park
2105 Highway 20
Sedro Woolley, WA 98284

Internet Sites

Canadian Wildlife Service
http://www.cws-scf.ec.gc.ca/cwshom_e.html

National Wildlife Federation—Ranger Rick's Kids Zone
http://www.nwf.org/kids

Index

DATE DUE
